Air Fryer Recipes

Disclaimer

Copyright © 2017

All Rights Reserved.

No part of this eBook can be transmitted or reproduced in any form including print, electronic, photocopying, scanning, mechanical or recording without prior written permission from the author.

While the author has taken utmost efforts to ensure the accuracy of the written content, all readers are advised to follow information mentioned herein at their own risk. The author cannot be held responsible for any personal or commercial damage caused by information. All readers are encouraged to seek professional advice when needed.

About the Author

Sam Kuma is passionate about sharing his culinary experience with the world. His work involves the modernization of healthy diet plans. He has published many recipe books for vegan, ketogenic, paleo diets and dash food cooking, along with several cookbooks on ethnic cuisines. His main focus is to make healthy diets like vegan and ketogenic mainstream by sharing easy-to-create and appetizing recipes. In his first two books regarding vegan recipes, he has produced delicious vegan chocolates, desserts, ice creams, burgers, and sandwiches.

Book Description

Air fryer recipes are the newest rage to hit kitchens around the world. An air fryer is designed to fry, bake and roast foods with the use of minimal fat. In this day and age where everybody is looking for ways to enhance their health, the air fryer proves to be an ideal option. It requires minimal effort to operate one but leaves you with maximum benefits.

There might be tons of air fryer books out there but none as good as this one. This book has been designed after much research conducted on the topic. The information and recipes provided in this book are designed to help people transition into using the air fryer.

The main aim of this book is to provide you with vital information required to operate the fryer and how you can use it to your advantage. Right from teaching you about the different parts of the fryer to its operation and the advantages of using one, there are chapters on all aspects that will help you get started with your fryer at the earliest.

The book is easy to read and has been divided into simple chapters that you can read through one by one. The chapters are easy to go through with each one explaining in detail the different aspects of an air fryer.

The recipes all make use of simple ingredients that are easily available. The recipes can be used as a blueprint to come up with some of your own.

I hope you have a great time reading this book and use the air fryer to enhance your health!

Table of Contents

Disclaimer 2

About the Author 3

Book Description 4

Table of Contents 6

Introduction 10

Chapter 1 – 15-Day Meal Plan 14

Chapter 2: Air fryer Breakfast Recipes 21

    Baked Ham, Mushroom and Egg 21

    Cheese Omelet 23

    Breakfast Burrito 25

    Cheese on toast 27

    Air Baked Eggs 28

    French toast Sticks 30

    Baked Eggs in Bread Bowls 32

    Easy Full English breakfast 34

    English breakfast 36

    Savory Toast 37

    Bell Pepper Oatmeal 39

Chapter 3: Air fryer Snack Recipes 41

- Cheese Spinach Balls 41
- Feta Triangles 43
- Rice and Cheese Balls 45
- Garlic Mushrooms 47
- Crispy Avocado Fries 48
- Potato Croquettes 50
- Chili Garlic Potato Wedges 52
- Tandoori Chicken Drummettes 54
- Baked Mini Quiches 56
- Mac & Cheese Wheel 58
- Cauliflower Buffalo Bites 60
- Samosa 62

Chapter 4: Air fryer Lunch Recipes 65

- Quinoa stuffed Mushrooms 65
- Air Fryer Burgers 67
- Saltimbocca Veal Rolls with Sage 69
- Turkey Breast with Maple Mustard Glaze 71
- Souvlaki with Greek salad and Tzatziki 73
- Chimichurri Skirt Steak 75

Portabella Pepperoni Pizza 77

Schnitzel Parmigiana 79

Meat Loaf 80

Gambas Pil Pil with Sweet potatoes 82

Fried tofu 84

Thai Fish Cakes with Mango Salsa 86

Chapter 5: Air fryer Dinner Recipes 88

Air fryer Mac and Cheese 89

Chicken Noodles 91

Stuffed Baked Potatoes 93

Meat Stuffed Courgette 95

Salmon Patties 97

Beet, Pumpkin and Goat Cheese Lasagna 99

Chicken Tikka 101

Asian Mixed Noodles 103

Fried Meatballs in Tomato Sauce 104

Lamb Roast 106

Spinach n Cheese Lasagna 108

Chapter 6: Air fryer Dessert Recipes 110

Gulab Jamun 110

Lemon Sponge Cake 112

Oreo Biscuit Cake 114

Peanut Cookies 116

Chocolate Covered Macaroons 117

Pumpkin Pie 118

Blueberry Custard 119

Peach Tarts 121

Apple Pie 122

Red Velvet Cupcakes 123

Blackberry and Apricot Crumble 125

Conclusion 127

Introduction

An air fryer is a simple machine used to fry foods without the use of oil. That's correct, the machine eliminates the use of oil to fry foods and crisps up ingredients just with the help of a little water. Introduced in 2010, the machine has since made its way into millions of kitchens worldwide and is set to grow in popularity in the years to come. The device is easy to use and helps in making nutritious meals using minimal ingredients.

The airfryer is a device that makes use of the Maillard reaction, which coats the ingredients with hot air. This air crisps up the ingredients from all sides and creates a thin brown coating. The device is capable of raising the temperature to up to 200 degrees Celsius thereby making it ideal to crisp up a variety of foods including tough meats.

The air fryer resembles a rice cooker and comes with three parts. The first part is the main machine that contains the motor, an exhaust, a cooling fan and a heating fan. This forms the bulk of the machine. The next component is the basket that will contain the ingredient for baking. The third component is the tray at the bottom that will catch any of the excess that drips from the ingredients.

The air fryer comes in many different sizes. You can pick the one for you based on the amount of utility that you wish to derive from it.

Phillips and Gowise are two of the most popular brands and sell quality air fryers. It has been designed ergonomically for efficient use. The handles are sturdy allowing you to pick up the basket with ease and attach it to the main machine. It also comes with a separator that allows you to cook many different foods at once.

Here is looking at some of the functions that the air fryer can take up.

The air fryer can be used to bake foods. You can do away with your conventional ovens as the fryer bakes foods with ease. The baking attachment that it comes with makes for the perfect utensil to use to bake all your favorite foods including cakes, cookies, and muffins.

The fryer can be used to roast foods. Right from vegetables to meats, you have the choice to roast an array of ingredients. All you need to do is cut it into small pieces and add it to the fryer. Choose the right temperature and timer and your dish will be ready in no time.

The air fryer can be used to fry foods. Frying in the fryer crisps up foods easily and produces the best result every time. Brushing just a little oil over the ingredients, or even a little water for that matter can help you remain with a crispy dish. The fryer crisps up foods by blowing hot air that sizzles up the ingredients.

The fryer can also be used to reheat foods, as well as thaw the ingredients. Add the ingredients to the basket and choose the appropriate setting. The fryer will take care of the rest.

The airfryer is the best choice for the following people.

- People on the lookout for healthier eating choices should switch over to using the airfryer. The air fryer helps in reducing the usage of oils and fats to a large extent. People must use just a small percentage of the fat that they generally use to fry foods.
- The fryer is ideal for bachelors that cannot cook as well. The fryer reduces the amount required to cook. All it takes is a little cutting and the fryer takes care of the rest. It eliminates the need to turn the ingredients around.
- New parents that are unable to cook lengthy meals can use the fryer to cook easy meals.
- Students who are new to cooking and learning the different cooking techniques.
- Elders who cannot spend too much time in the kitchen cooking meals.

This book will prove to be the ultimate guide for all those of you who wish to hop on the health wagon. You can get started as soon as you finish reading the book.

Chapter 1 – 15-Day Meal Plan

Day 1

Breakfast - Baked Ham, Mushroom and Egg

Lunch - Quinoa stuffed Mushrooms

Snack - Cheese Spinach Balls

Dinner - Air fryer Mac and Cheese

Desserts - Gulab Jamun

Day 2

Breakfast - Cheese Omelet

Lunch - Air Fryer Burgers

Snack - Feta Triangles

Dinner - Chicken Noodles

Desserts - Lemon Sponge Cake

Day 3

Breakfast - Cheese on toast

Lunch - Saltimbocca Veal Rolls with Sage

Snack - Rice and Cheese Balls

Dinner - Stuffed Baked Potatoes

Desserts - Oreo Biscuit Cake

Day 4

Breakfast - Air Baked Eggs

Lunch - Turkey Breast with Maple Mustard Glaze

Snack - Garlic Mushrooms

Dinner - Meat Stuffed Courgette

Desserts - Peanut Cookies

Day 5

Breakfast - French toast Sticks

Lunch - Souvlaki with Greek salad and Tzatziki

Snack - Crispy Avocado Fries

Dinner - Salmon Patties

Desserts - Pumpkin Pie

Day 6

Breakfast - Baked Eggs in Bread Bowls

Lunch - Chimichurri Skirt Steak

Snack - Potato Croquettes

Dinner - Beet, Pumpkin and Goat Cheese Lasagna

Desserts - Chocolate Covered Macaroons

Day 7

Breakfast - Easy Full English breakfast

Lunch - Portabella Pepperoni Pizza

Snack - Chili Garlic Potato Wedges

Dinner - Chicken Tikka

Desserts - Blueberry Custard

Day 8

Breakfast - Savory Toast

Lunch - Schnitzel Parmigiana

Snack - Tandoori Chicken Drummettes

Dinner - Asian Mixed Noodles

Desserts - Peach Tarts

Day 9

Breakfast - English breakfast

Lunch - Meat Loaf

Snack - Baked Mini Quiches

Dinner - Fried Meatballs in Tomato Sauce

Desserts - Apple Pie

Day 10

Breakfast - Bell Pepper Oatmeal

Lunch - Gambas Pil Pil with Sweet potatoes

Snack - Mac & Cheese Wheel

Dinner - Lamb Roast

Desserts - Red Velvet Cupcakes

Day 11

Breakfast - Cheese Omelet

Lunch - Fried tofu

Snack - Cauliflower Buffalo Bites

Dinner - Spinach n Cheese Lasagna

Desserts - Lemon Sponge Cake

Day 12

Breakfast - Baked Ham, Mushroom and Egg

Lunch - Chimichurri Skirt Steak

Snack - Samosa

Dinner - Chicken Tikka

Desserts - Blackberry and Apricot Crumble

Day 13

Breakfast - Air Baked Eggs

Lunch - Thai Fish Cakes with Mango Salsa

Snack - Rice and Cheese Balls

Dinner – Chicken Noodles

Desserts - Pumpkin Pie

Day 14

Breakfast - Easy Full English breakfast

Lunch - Saltimbocca Veal Rolls with Sage

Snack - Chili Garlic Potato Wedges

Dinner - Chicken Tikka

Desserts - Peanut Cookies

Day 15

Breakfast - Cheese on toast

Lunch - Turkey Breast with Maple Mustard Glaze

Snack - Cauliflower Buffalo Bites

Dinner - Meat Stuffed Courgette

Desserts - Gulab Jamun

Chapter 2: Air fryer Breakfast Recipes

Baked Ham, Mushroom and Egg

Prep: 10 mins	Total: 18 mins	Servings: 2

Ingredients:

- 8 small button Mushrooms, quartered
- 8 cherry tomatoes, halved
- 6 slices honey shaved ham
- 2 eggs
- ½ cup cheddar cheese
- 1 sprig rosemary, chopped (optional)
- Salt to taste
- Pepper powder to taste
- Salad greens to serve
- A little butter, melted, for greasing
- 2 whole wheat croissants

Method:

1. Grease the baking accessory or a baking dish, which is smaller than the air fryer with melted butter.

2. Place half the mushrooms and cherry tomatoes in the dish. Layer with half the ham. Sprinkle half the cheese. Repeat the above layer.
3. Make 2 small wells (cavities) in the ham layer. Crack an egg into each of the wells.
4. Season with salt and pepper. Sprinkle rosemary all over.
5. Place the baking dish on the basket of the air fryer. Place the croissants in the air fryer as well.
6. Bake in a preheated air fryer at 320°F for 8 minutes. After 4 minutes, remove the croissants. You can remove it earlier if you like it less toasted.
7. You can adjust the timing according to the way you like your eggs to be cooked. Set lesser time if you like the eggs runny or slightly more time for half cooked eggs or more time for fully cooked eggs.
8. To serve: Place the croissant on a serving plate. Place the baked ham and eggs over it. Serve with salad greens.

Cheese Omelet

| Prep: 10 mins | Total: 23 mins | Servings: 1 |

Ingredients:

- 1 large onion, chopped
- 2 tablespoons cheddar cheese, grated
- 3 eggs
- ½ teaspoon soy sauce
- Salt to taste
- Pepper powder to taste
- Cooking spray

Method:

1. Whisk together eggs, salt, pepper, and soy sauce.
2. Spray a small pan that is smaller than the air fryer and which fits inside the air fryer with cooking spray.
3. Add onions and spread it all over the pan and place the pan inside the air fryer.
4. Air fry at 350°F for 6-7 minutes or until onions are translucent.
5. Pour the beaten egg mixture all over the onions. Sprinkle cheese all over it.
6. Air fry for another 5-6 minutes or until the eggs are set.

7. Remove from the air fryer and serve with toasted multi grain bread.

Breakfast Burrito

Prep: 10 mins	Total: 18 mins	Servings: 2

Ingredients:

- 4 eggs
- ½ avocado, sliced
- 6-8 slices turkey or chicken breast
- ½ red bell pepper, sliced
- ¼ cup mozzarella cheese, grated
- Salt to taste
- Pepper to taste
- 2 tortillas
- 4 tablespoons salsa + extra to serve

Method:

1. Spray a small pan that is smaller than the air fryer and which fits inside the air fryer with cooking spray.
2. Whisk eggs along with salt and pepper. Pour into the prepared pan.
3. Place the pan in the air fryer. Air fry at 390°F for 5 minutes. Remove the pan from the air fryer. Carefully remove the egg from the pan. Cut into strips.

4. Place aluminum foil in the air fryer tray.
5. Place the tortillas on your work area. Place some egg strips, chicken or turkey slices, avocado, bell pepper and cheese. Spoon some salsa. Wrap it up and place it in the prepared tray with its seam side down.
6. Place the tray in the air fryer. Air fry at 350°F for 3 minutes.
7. Serve with salsa.

Cheese on toast

Prep: 5 mins	Total: 10 mins	Servings: 2

Ingredients:

- 4 tablespoons Branston pickle
- 4 slices whole wheat bread or multigrain bread, lightly toasted
- 4 tablespoons butter
- 4 tablespoons parmesan, shredded

Method:

1. Spread 1-tablespoon butter over each of the bread slices.
2. Spread a tablespoon of Branston pickle over the butter layer.
3. Sprinkle a tablespoon of cheese over each of the bread slices.
4. Place an aluminum foil sheet at the bottom of the air fryer basket.
5. Place the bread slices in the air fryer basket.
6. Air fry at 390°F in a preheated air fryer for 4 to 5 minutes.
7. Serve hot.

Air Baked Eggs

| Prep: 15 mins | Total: 30 mins | Servings: 2 |

Ingredients:

- 3.5 ounces ham, sliced
- 2 large eggs, refrigerated
- ½ pound baby spinach
- 1 ½ teaspoons olive oil
- 2 tablespoons full cream milk
- Salt to taste
- Pepper to taste
- Unsalted butter as required, melted

Method:

1. Grease 2 ramekins with melted butter.
2. Place a skillet over medium heat. Add oil. When the oil is heated, add spinach and sauté until it wilts. If there is excess moisture in the skillet, then drain it off.
3. Divide the spinach among the ramekins. Divide and place the ham over the spinach.
4. Break an egg into each ramekin. Pour tablespoon milk in each. Season with salt and pepper.

5. Air fry at 350°F for about 15 minutes or according to the way you like the eggs to be set.

French toast Sticks

Prep: 5 mins	Total: 12 mins	Servings: 2

Ingredients:

- 4 eggs, beaten
- 8 slices whole wheat bread
- ½ teaspoon ground cinnamon
- 1/8 teaspoon ground cloves
- 1/8 teaspoon salt
- 1/8 teaspoon ground nutmeg
- 4 tablespoons butter, softened
- Maple syrup to serve
- Cooking spray

Method:

1. Add salt, cinnamon, nutmeg, and cloves to beaten eggs and whisk lightly.
2. Apply butter on either side of the bread slices. Cut into strips of about 1 inch wide.
3. Dip each of the strips in the egg mixture and place in the preheated air fryer pan. Air fry at 350°F for 6-7 minutes. Place

as many as you can but do not crowd. You can cook in batches if necessary.
4. After about 2 minutes of air frying, remove the pan from the air fryer and spray the bread sticks with cooking spray. Flip sides and spray the other side too.
5. Place the pan back in the air fryer and fry for about 4 minutes or until golden brown.
6. Remove from the air fryer. Serve hot with maple syrup.

Baked Eggs in Bread Bowls

| Prep: 5 mins | Total: 25-30 mins | Servings: 2 |

Ingredients:

- 2 large eggs
- 2 tablespoons heavy cream
- 2 crusty dinner rolls
- 2 tablespoons fresh mixed herbs of your choice
- Salt to taste
- Pepper to taste
- Parmesan cheese as required, grated

Method:

1. Cut the top of each of the dinner roll. Set it aside.
2. Scoop out some bread from the dinner roll so that a hole is created. (It should be big enough to fit an egg.
3. Break an egg into each roll. Sprinkle some fresh herbs over it. Spoon in some cream. Sprinkle salt and pepper. Finally sprinkle cheese over it.
4. Bake in a preheated air fryer at 350°F for 20-25 minutes until the bread is toasted and the eggs are set according to the way you like it cooked.

5. After about 18 minutes of cooking, place the tops of the bread that were set aside in the air fryer and bake until brown. Let the stuffed roll and the top sit for 5 minutes.
6. Remove the rolls and place on a plate. Cover with the tops and serve warm.

Easy Full English breakfast

| Prep: 5 mins | Total: 20 mins | Servings: 2 |

Ingredients:

- 4 tomatoes, halved
- 4 chestnut mushrooms
- 1 clove garlic, crushed
- 2 chipolatas
- 2 rashers smoked bacon
- 2 eggs
- 3.5 ounces spinach
- Cooking spray

Method:

1. Take a pan that is small than the air fryer. Spray with cooking spray.
2. Place tomatoes, mushrooms and garlic in it. Spray some cooking spray over it.
3. Place the pan in the air fryer basket. Place the bacon and chipolatas in the basket.
4. Air fry in a preheated air fryer at 390°F for 10 minutes.

5. Meanwhile place spinach in a bowl. Pour boiling hot water over the spinach. Let it sit for a few minutes until it wilts. Drain the water and add spinach into the pan.
6. Make 2 cavities in the spinach. Crack an egg into each of the cavities.
7. Reduce the temperature of the air fryer to 320°F. Cook for a few minutes until the eggs are set as per your liking.
8. Serve hot.

English breakfast

Prep: 5 mins	Total: 25 mins	Servings: 2

Serves: 2

Ingredients:

- 2 eggs
- 4 medium sausages
- ½ a can baked beans
- 4 rashers un-smoked back bacon
- 4 slice multigrain bread, toasted

Method:

1. Place sausages and bacon in your preheated air fryer. Air fry for 10 minutes at 320 °F.
2. Empty the baked beans into 2 ramekins. Crack the eggs into 2 other ramekins.
3. Place the ramekins in the air fryer along with the sausages and air fry for 10 minutes at 390 °F.
4. Remove from the air fryer and invert on a serving platter. Place the sausages and bacon on it.
5. Serve immediately with toasted bread.

Savory Toast

| Prep: 5 mins | Total: 9 mins | Servings: 2 |

Ingredients:

- ½ cup chickpea flour
- 1 green chili, thinly sliced
- Water as required
- 1 tablespoon fresh cilantro, chopped
- 1 medium onion, finely chopped
- ½ teaspoon salt or to taste
- ¼ teaspoon chili powder
- 6 slices whole wheat bread
- A little oil to brush

Method:

1. Add chickpea flour to a wide bowl. Add about ¼ cup water and mix to get a batter of easily dropping consistency. Add more water if required, 1 tablespoon at a time and mix well each time.
2. Add rest of the ingredients except bread and mix well.
3. Place an aluminum foil on the bottom of the air fryer basket.

4. Apply the prepared batter on both the sides of the bread or dip it in the batter and immediately remove it and place on the air fryer basket.
5. Air fry at 350°F for 4-5 minutes in a preheated air fryer or until done.
6. Cook in batches.
7. Brush the batter coated bread slices with a little oil after a couple of minutes of cooking or you can use cooking spray too.
8. Serve with ketchup or a dip of your choice.

Bell Pepper Oatmeal

| Prep: 10 mins | Total: 17 mins | Servings: 2-4 |

Ingredients:

- 2 large bell peppers, halved lengthwise, deseeded
- 2 tablespoons cooked kidney beans
- 2 tablespoons cooked chickpeas
- 2 cups oatmeal, cooked
- 1-teaspoon ground cumin
- ½ teaspoon paprika
- ½ teaspoon salt or to taste
- ½ teaspoon black pepper powder
- ½ cup yogurt

Method:

1. Place the bell peppers with its cut side down in the air fryer.
2. Air fry in a preheated air fryer at 390°F for 2-3 minutes. Remove from the air fryer and keep it aside.
3. Mix together rest of the ingredients in a bowl.
4. When the bell peppers are cool enough to handle, divide and stuff this mixture into the bell peppers.

5. Place the stuffed bell pepper back in the air fryer and air fry for 4 minutes.
6. Serve hot.

Chapter 3: Air fryer Snack Recipes

Cheese Spinach Balls

| Prep: 15 mins | Total: 30 mins | Servings: 8 |

Ingredients:

- 1.3 pounds spinach leaves
- 1 cup mozzarella cheese, grated
- 1 cup bread crumbs or more if required
- 1 medium onion, finely chopped
- 1 teaspoon chili flakes
- ½ teaspoon salt or to taste
- 1 tablespoon garlic, grated
- ½ cup cornstarch
- Oil for brushing

Method:

1. Place spinach in a bowl. Pour boiling hot water over the spinach. Let it sit for a few minutes until it wilts. Drain the water and add spinach into the blender. Blend until smooth. Transfer into a large mixing bowl.
2. Add rest of the ingredients except cheese into the mixing bowl and mix until well combined.

3. Divide the mixture into 16 portions. Make balls of it. Flatten the balls, place a little of the cheese filling in it and shape into a ball.
4. Brush with oil and place in the air fryer basket which is lined with foil.
5. Air fry in a preheated air fryer at 390°F for 10-15 minutes or until they are crisp.
6. Fry in batches.
7. Serve hot with either ketchup or a dip of your choice. Serve 2 balls per serving.

Feta Triangles

| Prep: 40 mins | Total: 43 mins | Servings: 10 |

Ingredients:

- 10 frozen filo pastry sheets, thawed
- 1 cup feta cheese, crumbled
- Freshly ground black pepper
- Salt to taste
- 2 green onions, thinly sliced
- 2 tablespoons parsley, chopped
- A little oil to brush

Method:

1. Mix together feta, parsley green onion, salt and pepper.
2. Cut each filo pastry sheet into 3 equal strips.
3. Place a little of feta mixture on the underside of the strip.
4. Fold the corner of the pastry over the filling to form a triangle. Fold again to a triangle in a zigzag manner. Repeat until the whole strip is used up. Apply water in the last edge and press well. Each strip will give you one triangle.
5. Repeat with the remaining strips. You get 30 filled triangles in all.

6. Brush the triangles with oil. Place 4-5 triangles in the air fryer basket.
7. Place the basket in the air fryer.
8. Bake in a preheated air fryer at 390°F for 3 minutes or until golden brown.
9. Cook the remaining feta triangles in batches.
10. Serve with a dip of your choice. Serve 3 triangles per serving.

Rice and Cheese Balls

| Prep: 20 mins | Total: 35 mins | Servings: 8 |

Ingredients:

- 2 cups cooked rice, preferably overcooked rice
- ¼ cup sweet corn
- 2 cups paneer (fresh cottage cheese), grated
- 1 medium carrot, peeled, grated
- A few small cubes of mozzarella cheese
- 2 tablespoons cornstarch
- 1 green chili, finely chopped
- 2 tablespoons cornstarch mixed with ¼ cup water
- 1 teaspoon garlic powder
- Bread crumbs as required
- Salt to taste
- 1 teaspoon dry oregano or Italian seasoning

Method:

1. Mix together in a mixing bowl, paneer, rice, oregano, salt, garlic powder, and cornstarch. Mix until well combined.

2. Mix together in another bowl, carrots, cubes, corn, and green chili. Divide and make 16 portions of each. There should be at least 1 cheese cube in each portion.
3. Divide the rice mixture into 16 portions. Make into a ball. Flatten it slightly. Place a portion of the carrot cheese filling. Cover from all the sides to make a ball. Repeat with the remaining portions.
4. Place a foil in the air fryer basket.
5. Place breadcrumbs in a bowl. First dip the stuffed ball in the cornstarch mixed with water. Dredge the stuffed balls in the breadcrumbs and place in the air fryer. Spray some cooking spray over it.
6. Air fry in a preheated air fryer at 390°F for 10-15 minutes or until they are crisp.
7. Fry in batches.
8. Serve hot with either ketchup or a dip of your choice. Serve 2 balls per serving.

Garlic Mushrooms

| Prep: 15 mins | Total: 23 mins | Servings: 8 |

Ingredients:

- 2 dozen mushrooms, remove stems
- 4 teaspoons olive oil
- 2 slices whole wheat bread made into crumbs
- 2 tablespoons flat leaf parsley, finely chopped
- 4 cloves garlic, minced
- Freshly ground black pepper to taste
- Salt to taste

Method:

1. Mix together in a bowl, breadcrumbs, garlic, salt, pepper, and parsley.
2. Add olive oil and mix to get a crumble mixture.
3. Stuff this mixture in the mushroom caps and place in the air fryer basket.
4. Place the air fryer basket in the preheated air fryer.
5. Air fry for 8 minutes at 350°F.
6. Remove from the air fryer and place on a serving platter. Serve with a dip of your choice. Serve 3 mushrooms per serving.

Crispy Avocado Fries

| Prep: 15 mins | Total: 21 mins | Servings: 4 |

Ingredients:

- 2 eggs, beaten
- 2 large avocadoes, peeled, pitted, cut into 8 slices each
- 1 cup whole wheat bread crumbs
- ½ cup whole wheat flour
- Juice of ½ a lemon
- Salt to taste
- ½ teaspoon cayenne pepper
- ¼ teaspoon pepper powder
- Greek yogurt to serve
- Honey to serve (optional)

Method:

1. Add flour to a bowl and add salt, pepper, and cayenne pepper to it.
2. Place panko bread crumbs in another bowl.
3. First dredge avocado slices in the flour mixture. Next dip it in the egg mixture and finally dredge it in the breadcrumbs. Now place it in the air fryer basket.

4. Place the air fryer basket in a preheated air fryer and air fry at 390°F for 6 minutes or until they are golden brown.
5. Transfer avocadoes on a serving platter.
6. Sprinkle lemon juice over it and serve with Greek yogurt. You can drizzle honey if you desire.

Potato Croquettes

| Prep: 10 mins | Total: 18 mins | Servings: 4 |

Ingredients:

- 1 large potato, boiled, peeled, mashed
- 2 tablespoons parmesan cheese, grated
- A pinch ground nutmeg
- 1 tablespoon flour
- 1 tablespoon fresh chives, chopped
- ¼ teaspoon salt or to taste
- 1/8 teaspoon pepper powder or to taste

For coating:

- ¼ cup whole grain breadcrumbs
- 1 tablespoon vegetable oil

Method:

1. Mix together all the ingredients of the croquettes until well combined.
2. Divide the mixture and shape into balls or desired shape.
3. Mix together oil and breadcrumbs until crumbly.

4. Roll the balls in the breadcrumbs and place in the air fryer basket.
5. Place the basket in the air fryer.
6. Air fry in a preheated air fryer at 390°F for 8 minutes or until golden brown.
7. Serve with ketchup or dip of your choice.

Chili Garlic Potato Wedges

| Prep: 60 mins | Total: 72 mins | Servings: 8 |

Ingredients:

- 4 large potatoes, chopped into wedges
- 1 teaspoon ground cumin
- ½ teaspoon turmeric powder
- 1 teaspoon red chili flakes
- 2 teaspoons garlic paste
- 1 teaspoon dry mango powder
- 1 teaspoon salt or to taste
- Cooking spray

Method:

1. Mix together all the ingredients except potatoes in a small bowl. Rub this mixture over the potatoes. Let the potatoes marinate for at least 30-45 minutes.
2. Place the potato wedges in a preheated air fryer. Spray with cooking spray and air fry 350°F for 12-15 minutes or until done. Turn the wedges around a couple of times in between while it is frying.
3. Serve hot.

4. To serve as lunch, serve wedges with a salad of your choice.

Tandoori Chicken Drummettes

| Prep: 7 hrs. | Total: 7 hrs. 10 mins | Servings: 6 |

Ingredients:

- 1 dozen chicken drummettes make a few slits with a sharp knife
- 2 cloves garlic, peeled
- 1 inch piece ginger, peeled, chopped
- ¾ cup low fat yogurt
- ½ teaspoon chili powder
- 1 green chili
- ½ teaspoon salt or to taste
- Sliced onions to serve
- 1 teaspoon garam masala (Indian spice blend)
- A few drops orange food coloring (optional)
- Juice of a lemon
- A few lemon wedges to serve
- Cooking spray

Method:

1. Blend together in a blender, ginger, garlic, chili powder, green chili, yogurt, and garam masala to a smooth paste and set aside.

2. Mix together in a small bowl, lemon juice, salt and food coloring. Rub this over the chicken drummettes. Refrigerate for about 30 minutes.
3. Remove from the refrigerator and add the blended mixture over it, toss well.
4. Cover and refrigerate for 6-7 hours. Stir in between a few times.
5. Remove from the refrigerator an hour before cooking.
6. Place the chicken drummettes on the air fryer grill pan. Retain the marinade.
7. Air fry the drummettes in a preheated air fryer at 390°F for 10 minutes.
8. Brush the drummettes with the marinade. Spray a little cooking spray.
9. Air fry for another 3-4 minutes.
10. Serve with sliced onions and lemon wedges.

Baked Mini Quiches

Prep: 20 mins	Total: 15 mins	Servings: 8

Ingredients:

- 2 eggs
- 1 large onion, chopped
- 1 ¾ cups whole wheat flour
- ¼ cup milk
- ¾ cup butter
- 2 tablespoons oil
- Salt to taste
- Pepper powder to taste
- 1 cup cottage cheese
- ¾ pound fresh spinach, chopped

Method:

1. Preheat the air fryer.
2. Add flour, salt, butter, milk to a bowl and knead into smooth dough. Refrigerate for about 15 minutes.
3. Meanwhile, place a skillet over medium heat. Add oil. When the oil is heated, add onions and sauté until translucent.

4. Add spinach and sauté until spinach wilts. Remove from heat. Drain excess moisture from the spinach. You can squeeze out the excess moisture with your hands.
5. Whisk together eggs in a bowl and add cheese and spinach and mix well.
6. Remove the dough from the refrigerator and divide into 8 equal parts.
7. Roll the dough into a round, which is big enough to fit the bottom of the mini quiche mould.
8. Place the rolled dough in the moulds. Place spinach filling over the dough.
9. Place the quiche moulds inside the basket of the air fryer and place the basket inside the air fryer.
10. Bake at 350°F for about 15 minutes.
11. Remove from the air fryer. Remove the quiche from the moulds.
12. Serve warm or cold.

Mac & Cheese Wheel

| Prep: 30 mins | Total: 60 mins | Servings: 3-4 |

Ingredients:

- ¼ pound elbow pasta or any other pasta of your choice
- 1 tablespoon +1/4 teaspoon salt
- ¼ cup heavy cream
- ¼ cup whole milk
- ¼ cup Gruyere cheese, grated
- ¼ cup Fontina cheese, grated
- ¼ cup Sharp cheddar cheese, grated
- 2 tablespoons parmesan cheese, grated
- ¼ teaspoon Emerils original essence seasoning
- A pinch ground nutmeg
- Pepper to taste
- Salt to taste
- 2 tablespoons bread crumbs
- 1 ½ teaspoons unsalted butter, melted

Method:

1. Cook pasta with a tablespoon of salt according to the instructions on the package. Drain and place in a bowl.

2. Add the cheeses except Parmesan into the bowl of pasta. Also add milk, heavy cream, original essence seasoning, ¼ teaspoon salt, pepper and nutmeg and mix well.
3. Take a small baking dish that is smaller than the air fryer and fits well in the air fryer.
4. Place pasta mixture in the dish. Mix together in a small bowl, Parmesan, breadcrumbs and butter and sprinkle over the pasta.
5. Place the dish in the air fryer basket.
6. Air fry in a preheated air fryer at 350°F for 30 minutes or until golden brown.
7. Let it cool for 20-25 minutes. Invert on to a serving platter. Chop into wedges and serve warm.

Cauliflower Buffalo Bites

Prep: 10 mins	Total: 35 mins	Servings: 12

Ingredients:

- 2 large heads cauliflowers, cut into bite size florets
- 4 teaspoons garlic powder
- 2 tablespoons butter or coconut oil, melted
- Salt to taste
- Pepper to taste
- Olive oil cooking spray
- 1-1 ½ cups Frank's Buffalo wing style hot sauce or any other hot wing sauce

Method:

1. Mix together in a large bowl, garlic powder, salt, and pepper. Add cauliflower and toss well. Spray some cooking spray on the cauliflowers so that they are well coated.
2. Place a foil in the air fryer basket. Place the cauliflower florets on the foil.
3. Place the air fryer basket in the air fryer.

4. Air fry in a preheated air fryer at 390°F for 15-20 minutes or until golden brown. Turn the cauliflower half way through cooking.
5. Pour melted butter in a glass bowl. Add hot sauce and whisk well.
6. Add the roasted cauliflower and stir well so that the cauliflower florets are well coated with the sauce.
7. Place it back in the air fryer. Cook for another 5 minutes.
8. Serve immediately

Samosa

| Prep: 20 mins | Total: 55 - 60 mins | Servings: 3-4 |

Ingredients

Stuffing

- 4 medium potatoes, boiled
- ½ cup peas, boiled
- 1 ½ teaspoon gram masala powder
- 1 teaspoon ginger-garlic paste
- ½ teaspoon chili flakes
- ½ teaspoon turmeric
- A pinch of salt
- ½ teaspoon cumin seeds
- 2 tablespoon oil

For the coating

- 2 cups all purpose flour
- 1 teaspoon carom seeds
- 1-2 teaspoon ghee/butter, melted
- A pinch of salt
- Water

Method

For stuffing

1. Take a medium mixing bowl and add the potatoes and the peas to it. Mash them well so that no chunks are left.
2. Add gram masala mix, ginger-garlic paste, chili flakes, turmeric powder and salt to the above mixture.
3. Mix well.
4. Keep a saucepan on medium flames. Heat 2-tablespoon oil in the pan.
5. Add the cumin seeds to the pan. Once the cumin starts spluttering add the potato mixture to the pan.
6. Mix well and let it cook for a few minutes while stirring constantly.
7. When done, remove from the pan and keep it aside.

For coating

1. Take another mixing bowl and sift all-purpose flour in it.
2. Add carom seeds, ghee and water to the bowl.
3. Knead the mixture to form a firm dough. Cover it with a wet cloth and keep aside for half an hour to let it rise.
4. After half an hour make small balls of the dough and roll small tortillas. Cut these rounds in half.

5. Take one of the halves and place a small dollop of the potato mixture and fold it into a conical shape. Seal the ends with water.
6. When all samosas are done brush oil lightly all over them.
7. Keep the air fryer on preheat mode at 380°F for 5-7 minutes.
8. Place the samosas in the tray and cook for 18-20 minutes or till they turn light brown.
9. Serve hot with tomato ketchup.

Chapter 4: Air fryer Lunch Recipes

Quinoa stuffed Mushrooms

| Prep: 20 mins | Total: 27 mins | Servings: 4 |

Ingredients:

- ½ cup quinoa, rinsed, cook according to instructions on the package
- 2 tablespoons walnuts, chopped into small pieces
- 8 large mushrooms, remove the stems
- 4 button mushrooms, finely chopped
- ½ teaspoon chili powder or to taste
- Salt to taste
- Pepper powder to taste
- 4 tablespoons Parmesan cheese, shredded

Method:

1. Mix together in a bowl, cooked quinoa, chopped mushrooms, walnuts, chili powder, salt, pepper and cheese.
2. Stuff this filling in the large mushrooms.
3. Place the mushrooms in the air fryer basket.

4. Air fry in a preheated air fryer at 380°F for 7 minutes or until done. Cook in batches if necessary.

Air Fryer Burgers

| Prep: 14 mins | Total: 59 mins | Servings: 6 |

Ingredients:

- 1 pound mixed mince of pork and beef
- 1 ½ teaspoons garlic paste
- 1 medium onion, minced
- 1 ½ teaspoons tomato puree
- 1 ½ teaspoons basil
- 1 ½ teaspoons mustard
- 1 ½ teaspoons mixed herbs
- Salt to taste
- Pepper to taste
- 6 burger buns
- Salad to top the burger
- Cheese slice (optional)

Method:

1. Add mincemeat, onions, garlic paste, tomato puree, herbs, mustard, salt, and pepper into a mixing bowl.
2. Divide the mixture into 6 equal portions. Shape the portions into patties.

3. Place the burgers on the air fryer basket. Place the air fryer basket in the air fryer.
4. Air fry in a preheated air fryer at 390°F for 25 minutes. Now reduce the temperature to 350°F and cook for 20 minutes or until done.
5. Brush with oil if desired while frying.
6. Split the buns horizontally. Place salad of your choice on the bottom part of the burger. Place a burger. Top with a slice of cheese. Cover with the top half of the burger and serve.

Saltimbocca Veal Rolls with Sage

| Prep: 20 mins | Total: 25 mins | Servings: 6 |

Ingredients:

- 6 veal cutlets
- 1 ½ cups dry white wine
- 12 sage fresh leaves
- 2 ½ cups meat stock
- 6 slices cured ham
- Freshly ground black pepper to taste
- Salt to taste
- 2 tablespoons butter, softened

Method:

1. Add stock and wine to a saucepan and place the saucepan over high heat and boil until the contents have reduced to 1/3.
2. Season veal cutlets with salt and pepper. Place sage leaves over it. Roll the cutlets tightly.
3. Wrap a ham slice over each cutlet. Brush butter over it. Place the rolls in the air fryer basket and place the basket in a preheated air fryer.

4. Air fry at 300°F for 5 minutes. Fry the rolls in batches if necessary.
5. Add remaining butter to the hot reduced stock mixture. Add salt and pepper.
6. When cool enough to handle, slice the veal rolls. Serve with the gravy and steamed green beans.

Turkey Breast with Maple Mustard Glaze

| Prep: 10 mins | Total: 1 hour 4 mins | Servings: 3 |

Ingredients:

- 2 ½ pounds turkey breast
- ½ teaspoon salt
- ¼ teaspoon pepper powder
- ½ teaspoon dried thyme
- ½ teaspoon smoked paprika
- ¼ teaspoon dried sage
- 2 tablespoon maple syrup
- 2 teaspoons butter
- 1 tablespoon Dijon mustard
- 1 teaspoon olive oil

Method:

1. Brush the turkey breast with oil. Mix together the spices and herbs and rub the turkey breast with it.
2. Place the turkey breast in a preheated air fryer.
3. Air fry in a preheated air fryer at 350°F for 25 minutes. Turn it on one side and fry for 12 minutes. Next turn it on the other side

and fry for 12 minutes. The fully cooked turkey breast should show an internal temperature of 165 °F.
4. Meanwhile, add maple syrup, mustard, and butter to a bowl and mix well. Brush the turkey breast all over with it.
5. Air fry for 5 minutes.
6. Slice and serve.

Souvlaki with Greek salad and Tzatziki

| Prep: 45 mins | Total: 28 mins | Servings: 2 |

Ingredients:

For Souvlaki:

- 1 pound pork, chop into bite sized cubes
- ½ teaspoon paprika powder
- 1 ½ teaspoons ground cumin
- 2 tablespoons vinegar
- 1 tablespoon corn oil

For Greek salad:

- 1 small cucumber, chopped
- 2 ripe tomatoes, chopped
- 2 tablespoons Greek olives, sliced
- 1/4 cup feta cheese, crumbled
- 2 tablespoons wine vinegar
- 10 small green chili peppers (jarred)

For Tzatziki:

- ½ small cucumber, grated
- 1 pointed sweet pepper, halved

- 2 cloves garlic crushed
- 1 cup non fat Greek yogurt

Method:

1. To make Tzatziki: Mix together all the ingredients for Tzatziki. Cover and set aside.
2. For Souvlaki: Mix together all the ingredients for Souvlaki and set aside for at least 20-30 minutes to marinate.
3. Remove from the marinade and thread on to skewers and place in the air fryer basket.
4. Fill pointed sweet bell pepper with Tzatziki and place along with the skewers.
5. Place the basket in the air fryer.
6. Air fry in a preheated air fryer at 390°F for 8 minutes.
7. Meanwhile, make the Greek salad as follows: Mix together all the ingredients of the salad and set aside.
8. Serve Souvlaki with salad.

Chimichurri Skirt Steak

Prep: 2 – 5 hrs.	Total: 45 minutes + marination time	Servings: 2

Ingredients

- 1 ½ lbs skirt steak
- 1 ½ cup parsley, chopped finely
- 1/3 cup mint, chopped finely
- 1 ½ tablespoon oregano, fresh and chopped finely
- 4 garlic cloves, minced
- 1/2 teaspoon red pepper, minced
- 1 ½ tablespoon cumin, powdered
- 2 teaspoons paprika, smoked
- 2 ½ tablespoons red wine vinegar
- 1 teaspoon cayenne pepper
- Salt, as per taste
- Black pepper, powdered, as per taste
- 1/2 cup olive oil

Method

1. Take a large mixing bowl and slowly add all the ingredients given under the category of chimichurri and combine them. Mix well and keep aside.

2. Divide the steak into two equal parts and put them in a resalable plastic bag.
3. Put ½ cup of chimichurri mixture with the steaks in the bag and seal it. Shake well.
4. Keep the bag in refrigerator for about 2 to 5 hours. If possible leave it in the refrigerator for a day.
5. After the stipulated time, remove the bag from the refrigerator and keep aside for 30 minutes to bring it to room temperature.
6. Keep the fryer on preheat mode at 200 degree C for 5 minutes.
7. Remove the steak from the bag and pat them dry using paper towels.
8. Carefully put the steak in the cooking basket of the air fryer and let it cook for about 8-12 minutes. The steak should be medium-rare.
9. While serving garnish with some chimichurri.

Portabella Pepperoni Pizza

| Prep: 10 mins | Total: 16 mins | Servings: 6 |

Ingredients:

- 6 Portabella mushrooms, remove stems, cleaned
- 24 slices pepperoni
- 2 tablespoons olive oil
- ½ teaspoon dried Italian seasonings
- 6 tablespoons tomato sauce
- Salt to taste
- 1/3-cup mozzarella cheese, shredded
- 1/3 cup freshly grated Parmesan cheese
- ¼ teaspoon crushed pepper flakes

Method:

1. Brush olive oil over the mushrooms caps generously.
2. Sprinkle salt and Italian seasonings inside the mushrooms.
3. Spoon tomato sauce over the seasonings generously. Sprinkle Parmesan cheese over it.
4. Place a foil in the air fryer basket. Place mushrooms over the foil.
5. Place the air fryer basket in the air fryer.
6. Air fry in a preheated air fryer at 330°F for 1 minute.

7. Place pepperoni slices over the cheese and air fry for 3-4 minutes.
8. Sprinkle Parmesan cheese and red pepper flakes and air fry for a minute more.
9. Serve hot.

Schnitzel Parmigiana

Prep: 10 mins	Total: 30 mins	Servings: 2

Ingredients

- 2 pre-crumbed schnitzel, beef or chicken
- ½ cup parmesan cheese, grated
- 1/3 cup pasta sauce of your choice

Method:

1. Place the schnitzel in the air fryer basket.
2. Place the air fryer basket in the air fryer.
3. Air fry in a preheated air fryer at 350°F for 15 minutes. Remove from the air fryer and add pasta sauce over the schnitzel.
4. Sprinkle cheese all over it.
5. Air fry for another 5 minutes until the cheese melts.

Meat Loaf

Prep: 10 mins	Total: 35 mins	Servings: 8

Ingredients:

- 1 ¾ pounds lean ground beef
- 2 eggs, lightly beaten
- ½ cup salami or chorizo sausage, finely chopped
- 4 mushrooms, chopped into thick slices
- 2 tablespoons fresh thyme
- 1 medium onion, finely chopped
- 6 tablespoons whole wheat breadcrumbs
- 2 teaspoons freshly ground black pepper powder
- Salt to taste
- A little olive oil to brush

Method:

1. Mix together all the ingredients except mushrooms in a bowl. Knead to form dough.
2. Divide the dough into 2 and place in 2 baking accessories or baking pans. Using a spatula spread the mixture well.
3. Divide the mushroom slices and place on top of the meat in both the pans. Press the mushrooms slightly into the meat.

4. Brush the top with olive oil.
5. Place one pan in the air fryer basket and place the basket in the air fryer.
6. Bake in a preheated air fryer at 390°F 25 minutes or until brown. Remove from the air fryer and let it stand for 10-12 minutes.
7. Place the next pan in the air fryer and repeat step 6.
8. Slice into wedges and serve with a salad of your choice.

Gambas Pil Pil with Sweet potatoes

| Prep: 3 hours | Total: 3 hours 20 mins | Servings: 2 |

Ingredients:

- 3 large sweet potatoes, chop into slices
- 6 king size prawns, cleaned, deveined
- 2 stalks lemon grass
- 2 shallots, chopped
- 2 cloves garlic, finely sliced
- 1 red chili pepper, deseeded, finely sliced
- 3 tablespoons olive oil, divided
- ½ teaspoon smoked paprika powder
- 1 tablespoon fresh rosemary, finely chopped
- ½ tablespoon honey
- 1 lime, cut into wedges

Method:

1. Mix together in a large bowl, garlic, red chili pepper, garlic, onion, paprika, and 2 tablespoons olive oil.
2. Add prawns and toss well. Let it marinate for 2 - 3 hours.
3. Place sweet potatoes in a bowl. Add remaining oil, rosemary and honey.

4. Place the sweet potatoes in the air fryer basket and air fry at 350 °F for 15 minutes in a preheated air fryer.
5. Now fix the prawns on to the lemongrass stalks and place the prawns along with the lemongrass stalk in the air fryer. Increase the temperature to 390 °F for 5 minutes.
6. Serve sweet potatoes and prawns with lime wedges.

Fried tofu

Prep: 35 mins	Total: 60 mins	Servings: 4

Ingredients:

- 2 block firm tofu, drained, pressed of excess moisture, cubed into bite size pieces
- ½ cup rice flour or cornmeal
- 4 tablespoons cornstarch
- ½ cup parmesan cheese, grated (optional)
- Olive oil cooking spray
- Salt to taste
- Pepper to taste

Method:

1. Mix together in a bowl, rice flour, cornstarch and cheese. Add tofu and toss well so that the tofu is well coated.
2. Spray with cooking spray. Place the tofu pieces in a single layer in the air fryer basket.
3. Do not overlap. Cook in batches if necessary.
4. Place the air fryer basket in the air fryer.

5. Air fry in a preheated air fryer at 390°F for 25 minutes or until brown. Turn the tofu pieces after about 10-12 minutes of frying. Turn again if required.
6. Serve hot with a dip of your choice and a salad or soup.

Thai Fish Cakes with Mango Salsa

| Prep: 20 mins | Total: 27 mins | Servings: 4 |

Ingredients:

- 1 ¼ pounds fish fillets
- 1 egg
- 2 green onions, finely chopped
- Juice of 1 ½ limes
- Zest of 1 ½ limes, grated
- 1/4 cup flat leaf parsley or cilantro
- 5 tablespoons ground coconut
- 2 medium ripe mangoes, peeled, cut into small cubes
- 2 teaspoons red chili paste
- Salt to taste

Method:

1. Add fish, ¾ of the lime zest, egg, salt, 1 ½ teaspoon red chili paste, 3 tablespoons coconut and half the lime juice to the food processor and pulse until well combined.
2. Transfer into a bowl. Add cilantro and green onion. Divide the mixture into 15-18 equal portions and shape them into patties.

3. Place 5-6 fish cakes in the air fryer basket. Place the basket in the air fryer.
4. Air fry in a preheated air fryer at 350°F for 7 minutes or until golden brown.
5. Fry the remaining fish cakes in batches.
6. Meanwhile make the mango salsa as follows: Mix together in a bowl, mango, 1 teaspoon chili paste, a little cilantro leaves, remaining lime juice, and ¼ of the lime zest. Mix well and set aside.
7. Serve fish cakes with mango salsa and a salad of your choice.

A Short message from the Author:

Hey, are you enjoying the book? I'd love to hear your thoughts!

Many readers do not know how hard reviews are to come by, and how much they help an author.

I would be incredibly thankful if you could take just 60 seconds to write a brief review on Amazon, even if it's just a few sentences!

Please head to the product page, and leave a review as shown below.

Thank you for taking the time to share your thoughts!

Your review will genuinely make a difference for me and help gain exposure for my work.

Chapter 5: Air fryer Dinner Recipes

Air fryer Mac and Cheese

| Prep: 15 mins | Total: 30 mins | Servings: 3 |

Ingredients:

- 2 cups elbow macaroni
- 1 cup warm milk
- 1 cup broccoli or cauliflower florets, small florets of equal size
- 3 cups cheddar cheese, grated
- 2 tablespoons parmesan cheese, grated
- Salt to taste
- Pepper to taste

Method:

1. Place a pot over water over high heat. Bring to the boil. Add macaroni and broccoli or cauliflower.
2. Lower heat to medium and simmer until macaroni is al dente. Remove from heat and drain the water. Add it back into the pot. Add cheddar cheese, salt, pepper, and milk and stir. Transfer into an ovenproof dish that is smaller than the air fryer.

3. Sprinkle Parmesan cheese. Place the dish in the air fryer basket. Place the basket in the air fryer.
4. Bake in a preheated air fryer at 350°F for 15 minutes or until the pasta will bubble.
5. Let it rest in the air fryer for 8-10 minutes.
6. Serve.

Chicken Noodles

| Prep: 60 mins | Total: 1 hour 16 mins | Servings: 8 |

Ingredients:

- 1 ½ pounds chicken thigh fillets, chop into pieces
- 1 ¼ pounds udon noodles
- 1 ½ teaspoons sambal olek
- 2 red onions, chopped
- ¾ pound chestnut mushrooms
- ¾ pound shiitake mushrooms
- ¾ pound bean sprouts
- 4 cloves garlic, sliced
- 6 tablespoons soy sauce
- 4 tablespoons sesame oil
- 2 tablespoons sesame seeds
- ¾ pound glasswort
- A handful krupuks

Method:

1. Mix together soy sauce, garlic, and sambal olek in a large bowl. Add chicken pieces and toss. Set aside for at least an hour.

2. Meanwhile, cook noodles according to instructions on the package.
3. Drizzle about 2 tablespoons sesame oil over the cooked noodles and set aside.
4. Place the chicken pieces in the air fryer basket and place the basket in a preheated air fryer. Discard the marinade.
5. Set the timer for 16 minutes and fry at 390°F for 6 minutes. Flip the chicken pieces in between a couple of times while it is frying
6. After 6 minutes, add mushrooms, onion, bean sprout and glasswort and mix. Cook for another 5 minutes.
7. Add noodles and give it a good stir. Cook for 4 minutes. Add krupuk during the last minute.
8. Transfer into a serving dish. Sprinkle sesame seeds on top and serve.
9. Note: If you are finding it crowded before adding noodles, then remove half the vegetable mixture and set aside. Add half the noodles to the air fryer. Cook the remaining vegetables and noodles in the next batch.

Stuffed Baked Potatoes

Prep: 15 mins	Total: 41 mins	Servings: 8

Ingredients:

- 2 tablespoons butter, melted
- 8 medium potatoes, peeled, halved

For stuffing:

- ½ cup bacon, chopped
- 1 onion, chopped
- 2 cloves garlic, minced
- ¼ teaspoon salt or to taste
- ¼ teaspoon pepper powder
- ½ cup cheddar cheese, grated

Method:

1. Place aluminum foil in the air fryer basket.
2. Brush the potatoes with butter and place it in the air fryer basket.
3. Place the air fryer basket in the air fryer.
4. Air fry in a preheated air fryer at 350°F for 10 minutes. Brush the potatoes again with a little butter and air fry for 10 minutes. Remove from the air fryer.

5. When potatoes are cool enough to handle, scoop out the inside of the potatoes and set aside the potato cases.
6. Meanwhile, place a pan over medium heat. Add bacon, scooped potato, onion, and garlic and sauté until the bacon is cooked.
7. Remove from heat and add half the cheese, mix well. Cool for a while.
8. When cool enough to handle, stuff this mixture inside the potato cases.
9. Place the potato cases back in the air fryer and sprinkle the remaining cheese over it.
10. Air fry for 6-8 minutes. Remove from the air fryer and serve hot.

Meat Stuffed Courgette

| Prep: 20 mins | Total: 40 mins | Servings: 2 |

Ingredients:

- 2 large courgettes
- 2 cloves garlic, crushed
- 2 cups lean ground beef
- ½ cup feta cheese, crumbled
- 1 tablespoon mild paprika powder
- Freshly ground black pepper to taste
- Salt to taste

Method:

1. Slice off the ends of the courgettes. Slice each courgette into 6 equal parts.
2. Scoop out the flesh with a teaspoon leaving about 1 cm from the bottom and 1/2 centimeter from the sides.
3. Sprinkle salt inside the scooped courgettes.
4. Mix together rest of the ingredients in a bowl. Divide this mixture into 12 equal portions and stuff in the hollow courgette slices. Press well.
5. Cook the courgettes in batches.

6. Place a few courgette slices in the air fryer basket. Place the basket in the air fryer.
7. Bake in a preheated air fryer at 350°F for 20 minutes.
8. Similarly fry the remaining courgette slices.
9. Serve hot with cherry tomatoes for a complete meal.

Salmon Patties

Prep: 15 mins	Total: 40 mins	Servings: 6

Ingredients:

- 1.8 pounds russet potatoes, peeled, chopped into small pieces
- 1 cup frozen vegetables, parboiled, drained
- 0.8 pound salmon
- 2 teaspoons dried dill
- Salt to taste
- Pepper to taste
- 2 eggs
- 2 tablespoons fresh parsley, chopped
- Bread crumbs as required
- Cooking spray
- Mayonnaise to serve
- Lemon wedges to serve

Method:

1. Place a pot of water over medium heat. Add potatoes and bring to the boil. Simmer until potatoes are tender.
2. Drain the water and add the potatoes back into the pot. Place the pot over low heat until all the water in the pot dries up. Remove

from heat and transfer into a large mixing bowl. Cool and chill for 15 minutes.

3. Meanwhile, place the salmon in the air fryer basket and place the basket in the air fryer.
4. Air fry in a preheated air fryer at 350°F for 5 minutes or until brown. Remove from the air fryer and cool slightly. When cool enough to handle, flake the salmon with a fork and set aside.
5. Remove the potatoes from the refrigerator and add vegetables, salmon, parsley, dill, salt and pepper. Mix until well combined. Taste and adjust the seasoning if necessary.
6. Add eggs and mix well. Divide the mixture into 12 equal portions. Shape into patties.
7. Line the air fryer basket with aluminum foil.
8. Dredge in breadcrumbs and place in the air fryer basket. Spray with cooking spray.
9. Air fry in a preheated air fryer at 350°F for 12 minutes or until brown. Flip sides half way through cooking.
10. Serve with mayonnaise and lemon with a salad of your choice.
11. Serve 2 patties per serving.

Beet, Pumpkin and Goat Cheese Lasagna

Prep: 25 mins	Total: 1 hour 20 mins	Servings: 4

Ingredients:

- 3 pounds pumpkin, peeled, finely chopped
- 17 ounces mild goats cheese, grated
- 2.2 pounds beets, cooked, cut into thin slices
- 3.5 pounds red tomatoes, chopped
- 3 tablespoons fresh rosemary, torn
- 1.1 pounds fresh lasagna sheets
- 4 tablespoons olive oil
- 1 cup grana padano cheese, grated
- 2 onions, chopped

Method:

1. Place the pumpkin in a bowl and add about 2 tablespoons oil. Toss well and transfer it into the air fryer basket and place the basket in the air fryer.
2. Air fry in a preheated air fryer at 330°F for 10 minutes or until tender. Remove from the air fryer and cool slightly. Add the pumpkin into a blender. Also add onion, rosemary and tomatoes and blend until smooth.

3. Pour the blended mixture into a pan. Place the pan over low heat and heat the sauce for 10 minutes.
4. Grease 2 small ovenproof dishes with a little oil. Pour some of the sauce at the bottom of the dishes. Place a layer of lasagna sheets over it. Pour some more sauce over it. Lay some beet slices. Sprinkle some goat's cheese on it.
5. Repeat the above layers until all the ingredients are used up (retain some sauce and goats cheese for the topmost layer)
6. Finally sprinkle grana padano cheese over the goat's cheese.
7. Bake in batches.
8. Bake in a preheated air fryer at 300°F for 45 minutes.

Chicken Tikka

| Prep: 3 hours | Total: 3 hours 15 mins | Servings: 4 |

Ingredients:

For marinade:

- 2 medium tomatoes, deseeded, cut into 1 inch cubes
- 1 medium onion, quartered, separate the layers of the onion
- 2 cups thick yogurt
- 2 teaspoons turmeric powder
- 2 tablespoons chili powder
- 4 teaspoons cumin powder
- 4 teaspoons coriander powder
- 1 tablespoon ginger paste
- 1 tablespoon garlic paste
- 2 teaspoons salt
- 2 teaspoons garam masala powder (Indian spice blend)
- 2 tablespoons olive oil or any vegetable oil
- A few drops orange red food coloring (optional)

For chicken:

- 2 pounds boneless chicken, cut into about 1 ½ inch pieces

To serve:

- 2 medium onions, sliced into rounds, separated into rings
- Lemon wedges
- 2 tablespoons fresh cilantro or mint leaves, chopped

Method:

1. Mix together all the ingredients for the marinade and add chicken pieces to it. Mix well such that the chicken is well coated.
2. Cover and refrigerate for at least 2 -3 hours.
3. Remove from the refrigerator 30 minutes before frying.
4. Thread the chicken, onions, tomatoes, and bell peppers on to skewers in whatever manner you wish.
5. Place aluminum foil in the air fryer basket. Place skewers in the basket and the basket in the air fryer. Cook in batches.
6. Air fry in a preheated air fryer at 390°F for 15 minutes.
7. Turn the skewers in between a couple of times while it is cooking.
8. Remove on to a serving platter and place on a bed of onion rings. Garnish with cilantro and squeeze lemon juice over it.
9. Serve immediately.

Asian Mixed Noodles

| Prep: 15 mins | Total: 28 mins | Servings: 2 |

Ingredients:

- ½ cup cabbage, cut into thin strips
- 1 carrot, peeled, cut into thin matchsticks
- 1 large onion, thinly sliced
- 1 green bell pepper, thinly sliced
- 4 cloves garlic, minced
- 1 small packet brown rice noodles
- 1 cup tofu, cut into small pieces
- 2 teaspoons soy sauce
- White pepper powder to taste

Method:

1. Soak the rice noodles in hot water for about 7-10 minutes and drain. Break the noodles into smaller pieces.
2. Add rest of the ingredients to the air fryer and mix well.
3. Air fry in a preheated air fryer at 390°F for about 5 minutes.
4. Add noodles and toss well.
5. Air fry for another 8 minutes. Stir in between a couple of times.
6. Serve hot.

Fried Meatballs in Tomato Sauce

Prep: 15 mins	Total: 30 mins	Servings: 6

Ingredients:

- 1 ½ pounds ground beef
- 1 large onion, minced
- 1 tablespoons fresh thyme, chopped
- 2 tablespoons fresh parsley, chopped
- 1/3 cup whole wheat breadcrumbs
- 2 eggs
- Salt to taste
- Pepper powder to taste
- 2 cups tomato sauce of your choice

Method:

1. Mix together all the ingredients except tomato sauce in a large bowl.
2. Shape the mixture into small balls of about 1 - 1-½ inch diameter.
3. Place the balls in the air fryer basket and place the basket in a preheated air fryer.

4. Set the timer for 8 minutes and fry at 390º F degree C for 10 minutes. Do not overcrowd. Fry the meatballs in batches
5. When done, transfer the balls in a baking dish that is smaller than the air fryer and fits inside the air fryer.
6. Pour tomato sauce over it. Place the dish in the air fryer basket.
7. Reduce the temperature to 330º F degree C and cook for another 5 minutes.
8. Serve over cooked spaghetti.

Lamb Roast

| Prep: 10 mins | Total: 50 mins | Servings: 2 |

Ingredients:

- 1 pound lamb roast
- 1 large potato, chopped into chunks
- 1 bunch Dutch carrots, trimmed, peeled
- 1 small sweet potato, peeled, chopped into chunks
- 1 cup frozen peas, thawed, cooked
- 1-tablespoon instant gravy mix, cook according to instructions on package
- 1-tablespoon olive oil
- 2 teaspoons onion flakes
- 2 teaspoons crushed garlic
- 2 teaspoons dried rosemary
- Salt to taste
- Pepper powder to taste

Method:

1. Place carrots and potatoes on the baking accessory. Sprinkle salt and pepper.

2. Place the baking accessory in a preheated air fryer and air fry for 15 minutes. When done, remove from the air fryer and set aside and keep warm.
3. Meanwhile, mix together, rosemary, oil, garlic and onion flakes in a small bowl and rub this mixture over the lamb.
4. Place a small skillet over medium heat and add lamb. Cook until lamb is brown on all sides.
5. Remove from pan and sprinkle salt and pepper.
6. Spread a sheet over foil over the baking tray and place baking paper over it. Place the browned lamb over it along with sweet potato and potato.
7. Roast in the air fryer at 350°F for 20-25 minutes. Remove lamb from air fryer and place on the cutting board. When cool enough to handle, slice the lamb.
8. In case sweet potato is not cooked, bake for some more time until done.
9. Serve lamb with baked potatoes, sweet potato, carrots, cooked peas and gravy.

Spinach n Cheese Lasagna

Prep: 15 mins	Total: 50 mins	Servings: 2

Ingredients:

- 1 large onion, chopped
- 3 whole wheat dry lasagna sheets
- ½ cup parmesan cheese, shredded
- ½ cup ricotta cheese, shredded
- 3 cups spinach, frozen, thawed, squeezed of excess moisture
- 1 tablespoon butter
- 1 cup pesto sauce of your choice
- Salt to taste
- Pepper powder to taste
- 1-2 tablespoons Italian seasoning

Method:

1. Grease the baking accessory or baking dish that is smaller than the air fryer with butter.
2. Place a lasagna sheet at the bottom of the baking accessory.
3. Next layer with 1/3 the spinach followed by 1/3 the onions, 1/3 the pesto sauce, salt, pepper, and 1/3 the ricotta cheese.

4. Repeat the above layers twice more.
5. In the last layer, sprinkle Parmesan cheese on top. Cover the baking dish with a foil.
6. Place the baking accessory inside the air fryer basket.
7. Bake in a preheated air fryer at 350°F for 25-30 minutes. Uncover and continue cooking for 3-4 minutes.
8. Remove from air fryer and cool for 5 minutes before serving.

Chapter 6: Air fryer Dessert Recipes

Gulab Jamun

| Prep: 15 mins | Total: 20 mins | Servings: 10-12 |

Ingredients:

For jamun:

- 1 cup milk powder
- 1 cup milk
- 1 cup flour
- 2 tablespoons baking powder

For syrup:

- 2 cups sugar
- 2 cups water
- 1 teaspoon rose extract or a tablespoon rose water

Method:

1. Mix together all the ingredients of jamun and form smooth dough. Divide into 20-25 equal portions and shape into small

balls. Place the balls in the air fryer basket and place the basket in the air fryer.
2. Air fry in a preheated air fryer at 350°F for 5 minutes or until they turn golden brown.
3. Meanwhile make the syrup as follows: Pour water into a saucepan and place the pan over medium heat. Add sugar and bring to the boil. Stir until the sugar is completely dissolved.
4. Remove from heat and cool slightly. Add rose extract and stir. Add the fried balls in it and let it soak in it for at least an hour.
5. Serve warm or at room temperature but not chilled

Lemon Sponge Cake

Prep: 10 mins	Total: 25 mins	Servings: 6-8

Ingredients:

- 1-cup self-raising flour
- ¼ pound butter at room temperature
- ½ cup + 1 tablespoon caster sugar
- ½ teaspoon baking powder
- 2 small eggs
- ½ teaspoon lemon zest, grated
- A little melted butter for greasing the baking dish

Method:

1. Add all the ingredients of the cake into a blender and blend until smooth and creamy.
2. Grease a baking dish with melted butter. Pour the batter into the dish.
3. Place the dish in a preheated air fryer and bake at 350°F for 15 minutes or until a toothpick when inserted in the center comes out clean. Do not check before the timer goes off.
4. Remove the dish from the air fryer and let it cool.

5. Run a knife all around the cake and remove the cake from the dish.
6. Slice and serve.

Oreo Biscuit Cake

| Prep: 8 mins | Total: 16 mins | Servings: 6-8 |

Ingredients:

- 25 Oreo biscuits, ground finely
- 2 teaspoons baking powder
- 1 teaspoon baking soda
- 2 cups milk
- 2 tablespoons almonds, slivered

Method:

1. Add all the ingredients of the cake except almonds into a blender and blend until smooth and creamy. Transfer into a bowl. Add almonds and fold gently.
2. Grease a baking dish with melted butter. Pour the batter into the dish.
3. Place the dish in a preheated air fryer and bake at 390°F for 8 minutes or until a toothpick when inserted in the center comes out clean. Do not check before the timer goes off.
4. Remove the dish from the air fryer and let it cool.
5. Run a knife all around the cake and remove the cake from the dish.

6. Slice and serve.

Peanut Cookies

| Prep: 10 mins | Total: 22 mins | Servings: 12 |

Ingredients:

- 1 ¾ cups all-purpose flour
- ½ cup peanut butter
- 5 tablespoons vegetable oil
- A pinch of salt
- ¼ cup caster sugar
- 1 egg yolk, beaten

Method:

1. Add flour, peanut butter, oil, salt, and sugar into a bowl and mix well using your hands until dough is formed.
2. Line the air fryer basket with baking sheet.
3. Divide the dough and form small balls. Roll each ball into cookies and place on the baking sheet. Brush with yolk.
4. Place the basket in a preheated air fryer and bake at 340°F for 10-12 minutes.
5. If you like it crunchier, then bake for a couple of minutes more.

Chocolate Covered Macaroons

| Prep: 15 mins | Total: 34 mins | Servings: 8 |

Ingredients:

- 2 large egg whites
- 2 cups shredded coconut, unsweetened
- 1-½ ounces milk chocolate
- A large pinch salt
- 1 teaspoon almond extract
- ½ cup sugar
- 4 tablespoons butter

Method:

1. Place shredded coconut on a parchment paper lined baking sheet. Bake in a preheated air fryer about 4 minutes until lightly toasted.
2. Whisk egg white until frothy and doubled. Add sugar and salt and whisk again. Add almond extract and toasted coconut.
3. Divide and shape into small balls and place on the lined baking sheet.
4. Bake at 390°F for about 15 minutes until golden.

Pumpkin Pie

| Prep: 10 mins | Total: 50 mins | Servings: 6 |

Ingredients:

- 2 cups ginger snaps, ground
- 32 ounces canned pumpkin
- 1 cup egg whites
- 1 cup sugar
- 4 teaspoons pumpkin pie spice blend
- 2 cans (12 ounce each) evaporated skim milk

Method:

1. Grease an ovenproof pie pan with cooking spray. Place the ground cookies in the pan. Spread all over and press lightly.
2. In a large bowl, mix together the rest of the ingredients. Pour over the cookies.
3. Place the dish in a preheated air fryer.
4. Bake in an air fryer at 350°F for about 40-45 minutes. Remove from the air fryer.
5. Cool and refrigerate. Slice into wedges and serve.

Blueberry Custard

| Prep: 10 mins | Total: 35 mins | Servings: 4-6 |

Ingredients:

- 4 eggs
- 1 ¼ cups milk
- 1 ½ tablespoons butter, melted
- 2 tablespoons honey
- 1/3 cup all purpose flour
- ½ cup blueberries
- ½ teaspoon ground nutmeg
- 1 ½ tablespoons confectioners' sugar
- ½ teaspoon vanilla extract
- ¼ teaspoon salt

Method:

1. Add butter to a baking dish that is smaller than the air fryer and that fits into the air fryer. Swirl the dish so as to spread butter all over the dish. Alternately, you can grease ramekins.
2. Blend together eggs, honey, milk, vanilla, flour and salt until smooth. Pour in the dish.
3. Sprinkle blueberries all over.

4. Place the dish in the air fryer.
5. Bake in a preheated air fryer 390°F degree F for about 20-25 minutes until golden.
6. Remove from air fryer and cool for a while.
7. Sprinkle nutmeg and confectioners' sugar and serve.

Peach Tarts

Prep: 20 mins	Total: 50 mins	Servings: 12

Ingredients:

- 2 sheets (14 ounce package) frozen puff pastry, thaw according to instructions on the package
- ½ cup sugar
- 2 pounds peaches, pitted, chopped into wedges
- 2 tablespoons honey
- Freshly ground black pepper to taste
- A large pinch sea salt

Method:

1. Cut each puff pastry sheet into 6 squares of 4 inches each. Place the squares on a baking sheet that is lined with parchment paper. Prick the squares all over with a fork.
2. Place the fruit of your choice at the center leaving ½ inch border on all the sides.
3. Sprinkle sugar and pepper.
4. Place the baking sheet in the air fryer.
5. Bake in a preheated air fryer at 350°F for 25 - 30 minutes.
6. Sprinkle salt just before serving.
7. Drizzle honey and serve immediately.

Apple Pie

| Prep: 15 mins | Total: 65 mins | Servings: 4-6 |

Ingredients:

- 2 medium sized apples, peeled, cored, sliced
- 2 pie crust (store bought)
- ½ cup sugar
- 2 tablespoons unsalted butter, cut into small pieces
- ½ teaspoon ground cinnamon

Method:

1. Place one piecrust on a pie plate. Mix together cinnamon and sugar.
2. Lay the apple slices in layers over the piecrust in layers. Sprinkle sugar mixture over each layer and sprinkle a few butter pieces over each layer. Cover with the other piecrust.
3. Place the piecrust in a preheated air fryer. Bake in a preheated oven at 390 °F for about 10 minutes. Lower temperature to 350°F and bake for about 30 minutes.
4. Slice and serve warm.

Red Velvet Cupcakes

| Prep: 20 mins | Total: 45 mins | Servings: 12 |

Ingredients:

For cake:

- 6 eggs
- 1 ½ cups peanut butter
- 4 teaspoons beet powder
- 1 ½ cups icing sugar
- Cocoa 2 teaspoons
- 4 cups flour

For frosting:

- 2 cups hard butter
- 2 teaspoons vanilla essence
- 1 ½ cups icing sugar
- 2 cups cream cheese
- ½ cup strawberry sauce (optional)

For garnishing:

- A little chocolate crushed or shaved
- 2 strawberries, thinly sliced

Method:

1. Add all the ingredients of the cake into a mixing bowl and beat with an electric mixer. Pour into greased cupcake moulds up to $3/4^{th}$
2. Place the moulds in a preheated air fryer. Bake in an air fryer at 350°F for 5 minutes and then at 340°F for 10-12 minutes. Remove from the air fryer and set aside to cool.
3. For frosting: Whisk together with an electric beater, butter, icing sugar and vanilla until smooth. Add rest of the ingredients and whisk.
4. Top the cakes with the frosting and place strawberry slices and chocolate over it and serve.

Blackberry and Apricot Crumble

Time- 30-35 minutes

Ingredients

- 6 oz blackberries, fresh
- 20 oz apricots, fresh
- ½ cup sugar
- 1 ½ cup flour
- Salt, as per taste
- 2 tablespoon lemon juice
- 5 ½ tablespoon butter, cold

Method

1. Cut the apricots in half and remove reseed them. Dice the apricots in cubes and place them in a salad bowl.
2. Add around 1 ½ tablespoon of sugar, blackberries and lemon juice to the bowl and mix well.
3. Take an oven safe dish and grease it well. Pour the above mixture into this dish and spread carefully.
4. In another bowl add salt and flour and mix well.
5. Add the remaining sugar to the above bowl and mix again.
6. Add around 1 tablespoon cold water and butter to the flour mixture and knead. A crumbly mixture should form.

7. Keep the fryer on preheat mode at 200 degree c for about 3-5 minutes.
8. Spread the flour mixture over the fruits carefully. Press down lightly to set it.
9. Put the oven dish in the fryer basket and cook for about 15-22 minutes or until crumble turns golden brown.

Conclusion

Thank you once again for buying this book.

You now realize how versatile and remarkable the air fryer is. It is multi-purpose device that can help you cook healthy as well as tasty foods in no time.

Do follow the safety precautions and instructions when using the device. Try to clean the fryer frequently using the cleaning instructions given in the pamphlet that comes with your device. By cleaning the device regularly and by following the safety precautions, you will extend the life of your device many years. It will become your life long cooking partner.

Remember the recipes in this book are just guidelines, you can experiment with them to make your own recipes with your special touch! So what are you waiting for, get cooking!

Good luck and thanks again!

The end… almost!

Reviews are not easy to come by.

As an independent author with a tiny marketing budget, I rely on readers, like you, to leave a short review on Amazon.

Even if it's just a sentence or two!

So if you enjoyed the book, please head to the product page, and leave a review as shown below.

I am very appreciative for your review as it truly makes a difference.

Thank you from the bottom of my heart for purchasing this book and reading it to the end.